PUTTING ON A PLAY

THE YOUNG PLAYWRIGHT'S GUIDE TO SCRIPTING, DIRECTING, AND PERFORMING

by Nancy Bentley and Donna Guthrie

Illustrated by Katy Keck Arnsteen

The Millbrook Press • Brookfield, Connecticut

This book is dedicated to Alex and to all young people who want to see their stories performed on stage.

Science Experiments With Ben Franklin © Donna Guthrie
If I Had a Drum and *Song of the Open Road* © Jean Ciavonne
Adventures with Cool Cat © Katie Hubbs and Sarah Rogers
The Princess and the Stableboy © Lauren Johnson
Mr. Vanatoli and the Magic Pumpkin Seeds
© Donna Guthrie and Nancy Ekberg
Used by permission

Published by The Millbrook Press, Inc.
2 Old New Milford Road, Brookfield, Connecticut 06804

Library of Congress Cataloging-in-Publication Data
Bentley, Nancy. Putting On A Play: The Young Playwright's Guide
to Scripting, Directing, and Performing/Nancy Bentley and
Donna Guthrie: illustrated by Katy Keck Arnsteen.
p. cm.
Includes bibliographical references and index.
Summary: A step-by-step guide for the playwright including
suggestions for finding a story, writing a script, producing a play,
and performing it on stage. Includes sample plays.
ISBN 0-7613-0011-2
1. Playwriting—Juvenile literature. 2. Theater—Production and
direction—Juvenile literature. [1. Playwriting.   2. Theater—
Production and direction.]   I. Guthrie, Donna.
II. Arnsteen, Katy Keck, ill.   III. Title
PN1661.B44   1997
792'.023—dc20   95-47543   CIP   AC

TABLE OF CONTENTS

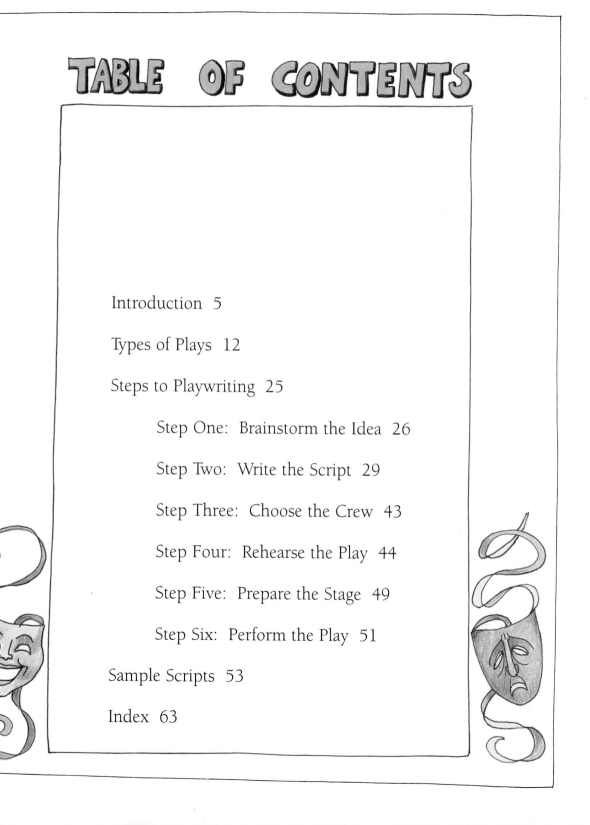

INTRODUCTION

Imagine yourself sitting in a theater. The lights go down. The curtain rises. The actors begin to speak and move. The action is happening right before your eyes. You are caught up in this story called a play.

The ancient Greeks were the first to formalize playwriting. By following a script, actors became the voices of their gods and goddesses as they performed on stage. Greek playwrights divided their plays into two types: comedy and tragedy. These two masks have come to symbolize the theater.

WHAT IS A PLAY?

A play is a story with a beginning, a middle, and an end. It is performed by actors in front of an audience.

A play offers the writer a chance to express a point of view about a topic he or she feels passionate about.

A play presents this idea through the actors' words, movements, and gestures.

A play is a blueprint for actors and directors. It can be interpreted differently each time it's performed.

A play is unique because of the live interaction between performers and audience. As people watch, they feel as though they are witnessing real events.

A play can be as simple as one person on stage telling a story or as complex as a three-act musical with full orchestra. It could happen in a big theater, in front of your class, or in your grandmother's back yard. All you need is a story worth telling, an audience, and a script. When you have a script, you can perform your play again and again.

WHAT IS A PLAYWRIGHT?

People who write plays are called playwrights. They take an idea or story they want to share with an audience, and they turn it into a script. It is the playwright's job to make the people in the audience believe the story is happening right before their eyes. The playwright does this by using dialogue and action.

Being a playwright is different from being an author in three ways:

1. You can view your play with the audience and observe their reactions to the play.

2. You can accept compliments and comments about your play immediately after the performance.

3. You can collaborate with actors and directors to change and strengthen your work.

HOW ARE PLAYS DIFFERENT FROM BOOKS?

A book is created by putting words on paper.

A play starts with words put on paper but is complete only when actors speak the words on stage.

A book is usually read by one person at a time.

A play is watched by many people at the same time.

In a book, the author may have hundreds of pages to describe characters, setting, and action.

In a play, the playwright has a limited amount of time to show the audience the characters, setting, and action.

A book uses the reader's imagination to make the characters come alive.

In a play, the actors bring the characters to life on stage.

A book can be read anywhere.

A play needs a stage and an audience in order to be performed.

YOUR PLAY

There's a story deep inside you
    longing to be told,
With characters both good and bad,
    some strong, some weak, some bold.
You are the playwright of this script.
    By writing each line down,
You direct the actors to move on stage;
    they're heroes, villains, clowns.
Behind the scenes the backstage crew
    must sew and paint and weave.
Use makeup, props, and lights and sets
    for a world of make believe.
Finally, it's dress rehearsal.
    Every line's just right.
Invite your family and your friends
    to come on opening night.
Beyond the footlights in the dark,
    the audience waits quiet and still.
When you hear the loud applause,
    it gives your heart a thrill.
And when the night is over
    and all have gone away,
You'll know they've heard your story,
    in this performance called a play.

PLAY POINTERS

The rules for writing a good play are the same
as the rules for writing a good story.

1. The play must have characters we care about.

2. The characters must have a conflict that is dramatized in the play.

3. The play must have a setting that shows the audience where and when the story takes place.

BEGINNING
MIDDLE
END

4. The play must have a beginning, a middle and an end.

5. The play must have dialogue that moves the story forward.

But a good play also has three elements that make it different
from a book:

 1. In a play, the characters' thoughts and feelings are shown through dialogue, movement, and action.

2. In a play, the characters live and speak in the present tense.

3. In a play, the audience is drawn into the story by actors who dramatize the playwright's point of view.

This book is a step-by-step guide to playwriting. It will help you find a story, write a script, produce a play, and perform it on stage.

STEP 6
THE
PERFORMANCE

STEP 5
THE STAGE
SETS

STEP 4
THE
REHEARSALS

STEP 3
THE CREW

STEP 2
THE SCRIPT

STEP 1
THE IDEA

TYPES OF PLAYS

Shakespeare once wrote, "All the world's a stage." That means that ideas and characters for plays are all around us. In our everyday life we have dialogue, conflict, and action. Playwrights often use these elements with their imagination to create a play.

Think of the story you want to tell and the way you want to portray it. Here are the types of plays that will be presented in this book:

- ⭐ pantomime
- ⭐ improvisation
- ⭐ skits
- ⭐ monodramas

- ⭐ readers theater
- ⭐ puppet plays
- ⭐ radio plays

- ⭐ adaptations
- ⭐ one act plays
- ⭐ full length plays
- ⭐ musical plays

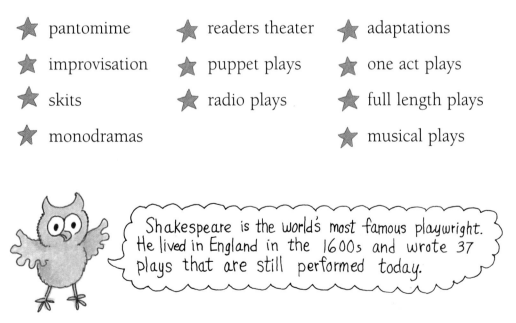

Shakespeare is the world's most famous playwright. He lived in England in the 1600s and wrote 37 plays that are still performed today.

PANTOMIME

In a pantomime you perform an idea, a feeling, or a story silently, using only movements and gestures.

Pantomime, sometimes called mime, was a form of early comedy created in ancient Greece and Rome. Clowns performed short plays that were stories from everyday life. Greek and Roman mimes used their voices. Today all pantomime is silent.

When you create a pantomime, choose a single idea, emotion, or event that can be expressed through gestures and movements. Separate each gesture and practice your movements one at a time. When you have memorized all the movements and can convey the idea, event, or feeling, you can add music to your pantomime.

Often mimes put on make up to exaggerate their expressions and gestures.

SUGGESTIONS FOR PANTOMIMES:

⭐ You're eating something sticky.

⭐ You've lost your money in the pop machine.

⭐ You've just received a letter; the news could be good or bad.

⭐ You're a baby learning to crawl and trying to talk.

⭐ Just before you go on stage for the school talent show, you rip the seat of your pants.

IMPROVISATION

> An improvisation is a situation for which the actors spontaneously make up the dialogue and action.

Improvisation uses no script. Words and actions are created on the spot. In rehearsals, actors often use improvisation as a way of warming up. They also use improvisation as a way of exploring their character's emotions and motivations.

For instance, you borrowed your best friend's new bike and someone stole it. Pretend you are at your best friend's front door. Ask someone to play your best friend in the improvisation. Now improvise what you will say and do.

SUGGESTIONS FOR IMPROVISATIONS:

⭐ Your alarm just went off and you don't want to get up.

⭐ You're suspended from school and you have to tell your parents.

⭐ You're getting your hair cut by a nearsighted barber.

⭐ You're making a cake recipe with a French chef who doesn't speak English.

⭐ You're waiting for a bus. You strike up a conversation with someone who looks remarkably like Dracula.

SKITS

> A skit is a short theatrical sketch that is usually comical.

Unlike an improvisation, a skit uses a script and is rehearsed. The characters interact to create conflict that usually ends humorously. In the 1920s, old-time Vaudeville was famous for its skits. These comical sketches were performed between the musical numbers and magic acts.

To write a skit, you must think of a funny situation where characters interact and create conflict.

SUGGESTIONS FOR SKITS:

★ Two people are sitting together in the bleachers, cheering for opposite teams.

★ You're eating dinner at your best friend's house and are served liver and onions, which you hate.

★ At your birthday party, your aunt has just given you the ugliest shirt in the world.

★ Someone has switched the signs for the boys' room and the girls' room.

★ Two kids both want the last seat on the bus.

MONODRAMAS

A monodrama is a one-character play.

Monodramas focus on a single incident or on an entire lifetime. They are often biographical. Unlike other plays, they do not always have conflict or a problem to solve. Instead, the monodrama gives the audience a bird's-eye view of the character's world and ends by providing a new insight. In a monodrama the actor can create other characters by using different voices, costumes, or props.

YOU CAN WRITE A MONODRAMA ABOUT:

⭐ a telephone conversation with your grandmother to tell her about your missing pet boa constrictor

⭐ a description of the time you got lost in Disneyland

⭐ the first time Ben Franklin flew a kite

⭐ your school's basketball team playing an NBA team

⭐ what your dog does while he's waiting for you to come home from school

⭐ an alien describing your family at dinner time

READERS THEATER

> In readers theater, actors read a story and turn it into a dramatic presentation. Lines are read rather than memorized.

In readers theater, performers select a story, poem, or chapter from a book that has lots of dialogue. The script is divided into parts for narrators and characters. The narrators read what is happening in the story while the characters speak the dialogue.

There are many different ways to present readers theater. One way is to read the script with no gestures or movements. Another way is to act out the script with simple gestures and props. Some performers like to memorize the lines and move about the stage.

TIPS FOR GOOD READERS
THEATER:

⭐ Choose an interesting story.

⭐ Divide the story into parts.

⭐ Type the story into script form.

⭐ Have each performer mark his or her part with a colored marker.

⭐ Rehearse enough so that you feel comfortable with the script.

⭐ Hold the script in a way that doesn't hide your face.

⭐ Read in a loud, clear voice.

PUPPET PLAYS

A puppet play uses puppets instead of live actors.

In a puppet play, dialogue is simplified and action is exaggerated. Because puppets cannot show expression, long speeches and songs won't work. Make sure that each puppet has a different voice so the audience can tell the characters apart. Almost any story can be turned into a puppet play, but it's helpful if the story is a familiar one.

When you write a puppet play, make sure all your dialogue and movement has a purpose. Decide where your puppet play will be performed and how many times it will be shown. Will you perform the play alone or with others? If you will perform by yourself, you can prerecord the dialogue. Keep in mind that you need a free hand for props and scenery. Remember, you can have only as many characters on stage as you have hands.

SUGGESTIONS FOR PUPPET PLAYS:

⭐ *The Fox and the Crow*

⭐ *Goldilocks and the Three Bears*

⭐ *Peter Pumpkin Eater*

⭐ *The Princess and the Pea*

⭐ *The Mouse and the Lion*

⭐ *Jack and the Beanstalk*

⭐ *There Was an Old Lady Who Swallowed a Fly*

Most puppet plays work best if they are no longer than ten minutes.

RADIO PLAYS

> A radio play is performed for a listening audience.

A radio play is built on good dialogue and imagination. The playwright supplies the words, the sound effects, and the music. The listener must add everything else.

Because a radio script is read, not memorized, it must be typed double-spaced to make it clear and easy to read. Put the characters' names in all capital letters on the left side of the page. Directions for how to read a part appear in parentheses after the character's name.

Remember to make your story simple and direct. Limit the characters to five and write your play in as few scenes as possible. Use sound effects when possible.

HERE ARE SOME IDEAS FOR RADIO PLAYS:

⭐ a mystery that takes place in the school cafeteria

⭐ a musical about Old MacDonald's Farm, complete with song and sound effects

⭐ an adaptation of Beverly Cleary's *Dear Mr. Henshaw*

⭐ an interview with friendly ghosts on Halloween night

⭐ a play about a grumpy school bus driver and his noisy passengers

⭐ a talent show of your friends telling their favorite jokes and riddles

MICROPHONE MANNERS

Keep these tips in mind when performing your radio play.

Each actor should have a microphone.

The microphone should be placed between the script and your face.

Stand about one foot away from the microphone.

Speak slightly to the side of the microphone, not directly into it.

Practice turning the script's pages quietly.

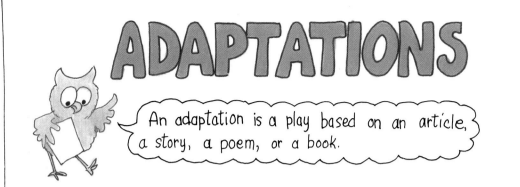

ADAPTATIONS

An adaptation is a play based on an article, a story, a poem, or a book.

Adaptations are fun to write. They give you a chance to take a favorite story, fairy tale, myth, legend, poem, or book and use your imagination to change it. Look for a story that has a simple setting, strong characters, and lots of action.

Make a list of the characters you want to use. Divide the story into a beginning, a middle, and an end. Look for the dialogue that is crisp, clear, and moves the story along. Change dialogue that doesn't work.

SUGGESTIONS FOR ADAPTATIONS:

⭐ Roald Dahl's *Charlie and the Chocolate Factory*

⭐ *Cinderella*

⭐ Your favorite R. L. Stine book

⭐ Your favorite short story from a magazine

⭐ The poem "The Night Before Christmas"

⭐ The Greek myth "King Midas and the Golden Touch"

ONE ACT PLAYS

A one act play shows a single incident in a character's life.

In a one act play, characters come together at a single time and place to experience a significant event. This all happens in one act. Conflict often occurs when they interact. The one act play usually has a small cast. Dialogue is brief and actions simple, but there is a clear beginning, middle, and end.

INCIDENTS THAT MIGHT MAKE
A GOOD ONE ACT PLAY:

★ a robbery at your corner grocery store

★ a backstage meeting with your favorite rock star

★ a meeting with you, your math teacher, and your mother

★ a conversation with your guardian angel, who becomes visible for just 15 minutes

★ the time your friend loses the tickets your parents gave you to the all-star game

★ the day your little brother finds a winning lottery ticket and wants to know what to do with it

★ the night you're babysitting the neighbor's kids and the lights go out in the house

★ the day you get stuck on an elevator with the school bully

FULL LENGTH PLAYS

A full length play shows characters' goals and conflicts through a number of incidents or actions.

A full length play is a long and more complicated type of play. It is usually two or three acts long. It is full of details about the characters, theme, and conflict. The main conflict starts early in the play and grows in complexity. Subplots or secondary stories can also occur throughout the play.

A full length play allows the playwright to develop the main characters' personality, goals, and obstacles to a greater extent. Each incident builds conflict and tension and forces the characters toward a climax that is the turning point in the story.

YOU MAY WANT TO SEE OR READ
THE FOLLOWING FULL LENGTH PLAYS:

★ *Romeo and Juliet*
★ *The Best Christmas Pageant Ever*
★ *The Princess and the Pea*
★ *Charlotte's Web*
★ *The Velveteen Rabbit*

MUSICAL PLAYS

In a musical play, the story is told through dialogue, music, and dance.

A musical is like a full length play. It contains interesting characters, themes, and conflict. But in musicals, the characters sing and dance as well as speak their dialogue. Songs grow out of a character's emotions such as love, anger, and happiness.

The main and supporting characters become soloists. The chorus is a group of characters that gives the audience more information about the story and the main characters.

In a musical, the music moves the story along. Most musicals leave the audience feeling upbeat and inspired.

TO WRITE A SIMPLE MUSICAL:

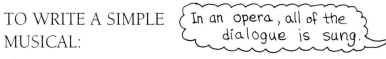

In an opera, all of the dialogue is sung.

☆ Choose a simple story.

☆ Write a script, placing songs at important emotional moments.

☆ Write some of the dialogue in rhyme so you can turn it into a song.

☆ Create a different melody for each character.

☆ If you can't write music, take a familiar tune and change the words.

STEPS TO PLAYWRITING

A playwright is an artist using a palette of characters, dialogue, and conflict to paint a story on an empty stage. This make-believe world comes alive when the playwright adds actors and costumes, and sets and props.

Approach your play one step at a time. Find a good idea, write the script, and choose people to help you. Design the set, rehearse, and perform the play.

To make a play of your own, just follow these steps:

Step 1
BRAINSTORM
THE IDEA

Step 2
WRITE THE
SCRIPT

Step 3
CHOOSE
THE CREW

Step 4
REHEARSE
THE PLAY

Step 5
PREPARE
THE STAGE

Step 6
PERFORM
THE PLAY

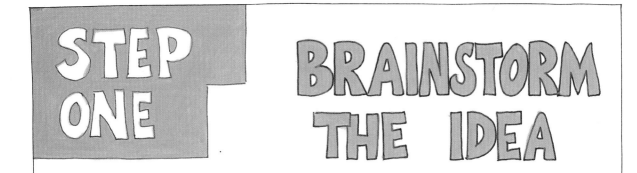

STEP ONE

BRAINSTORM THE IDEA

As a playwright, you have the opportunity to stand up and speak out about things that are important to you. You can promote something you believe in or examine an idea you're against. But before you speak out, you must look within and examine yourself:

⭐ What do I believe in?

⭐ What is important to me?

⭐ What would I stand up and fight for?

⭐ What do I like or dislike?

⭐ What are my standards?

⭐ What human traits do I admire?

Each one of these ideas could be the subject of a play.

You can get play ideas from your life and the people around you. Ask yourself:

1. Who are the people most important to me?

2. What's happened to me that's unusual or interesting?

3. What's my biggest problem?

4. What's my greatest dream?

5. What do I like to read?

6. What's unique about me?

Look at the world:

Ideas can also come from:

1. What people in the world do you admire?

1. NEWSPAPERS

2. What things scare you about the world?

2. TELEVISION

3. What interests you most about today's world?

3. RADIO

STEP TWO

WRITE THE SCRIPT

There are a number of ways to start a play. You can start with:

★ a theme

★ a situation

★ a character

THEME

A theme is the broad idea that the playwright believes and wants to share with the audience. It could be a global issue, such as world peace, or a personal issue, such as the importance of friendship. For instance:

You believe that kids should be paid well for doing chores.

You are interested in saving the bald eagle.

For a beginning playwright, it's easiest to begin with a situation.

SITUATION

A situation is a physical or emotional event. It could be something that happens to your main character at the start of the play. It could be a large event that affects society. For instance:

Your cat has just had ten kittens. Your mother says you must give them all away.

Your whole city is flooded and you need to go out for food and supplies.

CONFLICT

Conflict is the engine of your play. It is a clash between two opposing forces. Develop one conflict as the center of your play. Show it early by bringing together two characters with opposing goals. One will win and one will lose.

Conflict can:

 create issues and raise questions

change characters by making them struggle

express the playwright's point of view about the character's main problem and possible solutions

provide a plan for what happens in the play

ACTION

Actions are the characters' movements on stage. Without it your play would be boring. Action can also show character traits. In a play about the three little pigs, when the wolf blows the straw house down the audience sees that the wolf is a bully.

In *The Three Billy Goats Gruff*, the troll threatens to eat the billy goat time and again, but doesn't do it. In the end, the greedy troll is outsmarted when he faces the Big Billy Goat Gruff.

Conflict creates complex and realistic characters.

CHARACTERS
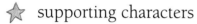

Characters are the people represented in a play. Playwrights create colorful characters in all sizes and shapes. Even when your play is about a situation or theme, it is the relationship between the characters that makes your play come alive.

There are three types of characters:

⭐ protagonists

⭐ antagonists

⭐ supporting characters

PROTAGONIST

The protagonist is the main character in the play. All the action that occurs is about the protagonist achieving his or her goal. The audience identifies with this character.

The main character must have a goal that is difficult to achieve. Throughout the play the main character must work hard for it. By the end of the play the main character usually changes and learns something along the way.

For instance, the goal of young Arthur is to pull the sword from the stone. Jack wants to steal the gold from the giant, and Dorothy wants to leave Oz and go home.

Before you begin to write your play, ask yourself these questions about your protagonist. Jot down your answers in a notebook.

⭐ Is your protagonist male or female?

⭐ How old is your protagonist?

⭐ What does your protagonist look like?

⭐ Where does your protagonist live?

⭐ Is your protagonist's goal clear? What is it?

⭐ Does your protagonist have a plan to achieve this goal?

⭐ How does he or she respond to obstacles?

⭐ Does your protagonist change by the end of the play?

⭐ What will happen if your protagonist doesn't achieve the goal?

ANTAGONIST

The antagonist, or villain, is the character who works against the protagonist. He or she does this by interfering with the main character's wishes, goals, or actions.

Ask yourself these questions about the antagonist or villain and write the answers in your notebook.

★ Is your antagonist male or female?

★ How old is your antagonist?

★ What does your antagonist look like?

★ Where does your antagonist live?

★ Is your antagonist's goal clear? What is it?

★ Does your antagonist have a plan to achieve this goal?

★ What is the antagonist's reason for opposing the main character?

★ What does the antagonist do to show his or her opposition?

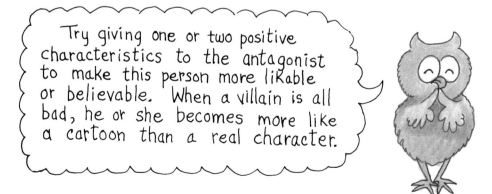

Try giving one or two positive characteristics to the antagonist to make this person more likable or believable. When a villain is all bad, he or she becomes more like a cartoon than a real character.

SUPPORTING CHARACTERS

Supporting characters are minor characters in the play. What they say and do helps the audience learn more about the main characters and the story. Often they are friends or allies of the protagonist or the antagonist.

Ask yourself these questions about the supporting characters and write the answers in your notebook.

⭐ Are your supporting characters male or female?

⭐ How old are your supporting characters?

⭐ What do your supporting characters look like?

⭐ Where do your supporting characters live?

⭐ Are all the supporting characters needed in the play? If not, can some of their traits be combined into one character?

⭐ Are the supporting characters different from one another?

⭐ Are the supporting characters friends or enemies of the protagonist?

DIALOGUE

Now that you know your characters, it's time to make them talk. What your characters say is called dialogue. They may have conversations with other characters or just talk to themselves.

Good dialogue can:

⭐ show the personality of each character

⭐ show conflict

⭐ express the playwright's personal beliefs

⭐ stimulate the audience's imagination

⭐ move the story along

Unlike everyday conversation, dialogue is short, concise, and to the point.

DIALOGUE DON'TS

- ⭐ Avoid junk words. These are words that are not specific and don't tell anything about the character.

- ⭐ Avoid cliches. A cliche is sentence or phrase that is so common that it's unoriginal.

- ⭐ Avoid long, rambling speeches. Try to keep each speech as brief as possible.

- ⭐ Avoid complex sentences.

- ⭐ Avoid needless repetitions that don't give any new information.

- ⭐ Avoid writing dialogue using only the past tense. Try to write it in the present tense—like real speech.

If you want the actor to say a line of dialogue in a special or particular way, write it this way:

WOLF: (*sweetly*) Where are you going, little girl, with that big basket?

RED RIDING HOOD: (*fearfully*) I'm going to my grandmother's house.

SETTING

Setting establishes where and when your story takes place. It gives your characters a time and place where they can interact and where things can happen.

To help create a setting, ask yourself these questions and jot the answers down in your notebook.

⭐ Where do your characters live?

⭐ Does the play take place in the past, the present, or the future?

⭐ Does the setting need to change in the play?

⭐ Is the setting big enough for characters to move about and for things to happen?

To save time and money, try to create a setting that will allow you the greatest flexibility when creating your sets.

SETS

Sets are the props and scenery that represent a setting on stage. For instance, the setting for *Little Red Riding Hood* would be Grandma's house in the woods. The set for *Little Red Riding Hood* could include a painted backdrop of trees, Grandma's bed, and a door for the characters to enter and exit.

PLOT: THE PLAY'S ROADMAP

Some plays are divided into acts which may be made up of several scenes. A scene is a small unit of action where something happens, a conflict arises, or a new situation is set up.

To guide you through the writing of scenes and acts, you'll need a roadmap. This roadmap is called a plot. It is the plan for the characters' actions, reactions, and events. It shows the forward motion of the play.

From the earliest scenes in the play the audience must see conflict between the protagonist and the antagonist. As the scenes unfold, tension builds. The biggest conflict, called the climax, occurs when all seems lost and the protagonist has one last chance to "save the day."

The climax is the most dramatic scene in the play where one character will win, conflict will be resolved, and the play will end.

Plot can be divided into three basic parts:

BEGINNING   MIDDLE   CLIMAX   END

To add excitement and urgency to the first scene, imagine an incident has happened off-stage before the play begins. As the play begins we see the characters reacting to this event.

1. Part one usually introduces the setting, the protagonist, and his or her goal.

   In Part one of *The Three Billy Goats Gruff*, we're introduced to the three goat brothers and learn of their goal to cross the bridge and eat the sweet grass on the other side.

2. In Part two the action begins. The main character meets the antagonist and learns of the obstacles he or she will have to overcome. This is the longest part of the play because problems will increase right up to the climax.

   In *The Three Billy Goats Gruff*, we meet the ugly troll and learn how he plans to stop the goats. The tension builds as each goat crosses the bridge. The climax is when the troll meets the biggest Billy Goat Gruff.

3. Part three is the ending of the play and follows the climax.

   Balance may be restored if the main character attains his goal. In *The Three Billy Goats Gruff*, the troll loses and the three Billy Goats Gruff are safe on the other side of the bridge.

SCRIPT FORMAT

A script is a list of all the characters, their descriptions, dialogue, movements, and stage directions. It also includes the number of scenes or acts included in the play.

One page of script equals about one minute of time on stage.

The beginning of the script consists of a title page with the title of the play centered and in capital letters, a page listing the cast, and a page describing the setting. Do not number these first pages.

Page count begins with the first page of the actual script. Number each page in the upper right-hand corner. You can also include a key word from the title.

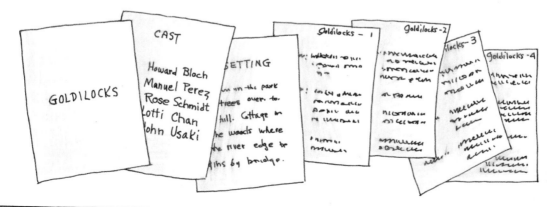

Describe the time and place for each act or scene.

SETTING

We're inside a cozy cottage early in the morning. A table is set with three bowls of porridge; one small, one medium, and one large.

Actor directions are short phrases intended for the person playing the role. Place them in parentheses under the characters' names and indented from the left margin.

GOLDILOCKS
(GOLDILOCKS knocks once on the door and then barges in.)

Character names are typed all in capital letters.

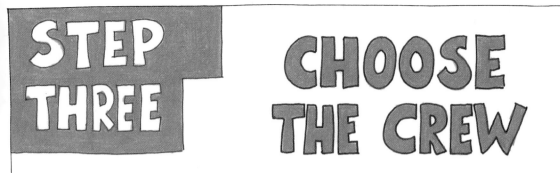

STEP THREE
CHOOSE THE CREW

If you choose to produce a play that uses sets and has several characters, you'll need help. You'll be working with other talented people who enjoy painting sets, designing costumes, and acting. As a playwright, it's important to remain open to their thoughts and ideas about your play.

The *producer* makes all the arrangements for the entire production by organizing the people and the equipment.

The *director* interprets the script, designs the stage movements, and works with the actors on dialogue and action.

The *stage manager* is responsible for the smooth and efficient running of each and every performance. He or she assists the director during rehearsal by supervising the lights, costumes, props, and sets.

The *actors* perform the script and make the play come to life.

The *makeup artists* help the actors with their stage makeup and hair.

The *stage hands* move the sets, organize the props, and manage the lighting, music, and sound effects.

The *set designer* creates and makes the sets for the stage.

The *costume designer* creates and makes the costumes.

STEP FOUR

REHEARSE THE PLAY

Once your play is ready, make several copies of the script. The producer, the director, the actors, the stage manager, and the technical crew will each need a copy.

AUDITIONS

If you do not have enough people for your play, consider asking an actor to play two parts. This is called "doubling."

Announce that you will have tryouts for your play at a certain date and time. You may want to use the school auditorium, a classroom, or the basement or garage of your house to hold your auditions.

At the first meeting, introduce the play. Tell about the characters and the technical jobs that need to be filled. Pass out a schedule of rehearsal times and the date of the performance.

Ask each person who wants a part to prepare a three minute monologue. Listen to the monologues one at a time before making a decision. If you can't decide, create a "call-back" by asking certain people to return to read again. Post your decisions or call the actors to tell them which part they have.

REHEARSALS

The first rehearsal is called a read-through. The director is in charge. Begin the rehearsal by asking the actors to read through the entire play while everyone listens.

In the first few rehearsals, you'll be working on memorizing the lines, working out the blocking (explained on page 47), and stage business.

The working rehearsals can be broken down into the following steps:

Divide the script into sections. A "beat" is a small section in a play, much like the chapter of a book.

Work on a beat by experimenting with different ways to say dialogue, move on stage, and handle the props.

After you've found movements and props that work, ask the actors to note them on their scripts. This is called "blocking." The handling of props is called "stage business." The stage manager keeps a copy of the script that includes all the blocking and stage business.

At the next rehearsal, ask the actors to say the lines from memory. This is called "running the lines."

Now do the same scene with lines, blocking, and stage business. This is called "doing the scene on its feet."

Repeat this process with other beats until your actors have memorized the entire script.

Add props to the set.

Go through the entire play without comments from the director. This is called a "run-through."

Have a technical rehearsal by adding lighting, music, and sound.

Add costumes and makeup for the dress rehearsal.

Give your performance.

BLOCKING

Blocking is a theatrical word for movement. On stage the actors must move among the props and the scenery. If the props and scenery are not ready when you begin to rehearse, mark their positions on stage so the actors can practice moving around them.

The actors' movements and place on stage emphasize the importance of the characters. Every movement an actor makes should have a reason. Center stage is closest to the audience, and is considered the strongest place to be. Getting up or standing is usually more powerful than sitting down.

A stage can be divided into parts. These symbols will help when you block your play:

Don't turn your back on the audience.

U - Upstage
D - Downstage
R - Right
L - Left
C - Center

Moving downstage means moving closer to the audience. Moving upstage means moving away from the audience. Right and left are labeled from the point of view of the actor, not the audience.

ACTING

It is the actor's job to make the character come alive on stage. As an actor, you must trust your feelings. The director can tell you what he or she wants, but not how to do it. You must breathe life into your character by becoming the character on stage.

During rehearsals, actors memorize lines and blocking. Here are some tips on how to memorize your lines:

⭐ Read the lines slowly.

⭐ Make sure you understand what the character is saying.

⭐ Make sure you understand what the character is feeling.

⭐ Read your lines with another actor. Listen to the lines that come before and after yours.

⭐ Break up a speech by dividing it into parts. Start with the first line.

⭐ Keep repeating this line until you're sure of it.

⭐ Always remember why you're saying the line and what the words mean.

⭐ After you memorize this line, move on one line at a time until you have memorized your entire part.

An understudy is someone who is prepared to fill in for an actor who cannot perform.

Before the actors rehearse on stage, the set designers and technical crew should decide what each set will look like. Some sets are realistic and some just suggest the feeling of a place. The technical crew is in charge of painting the sets, experimenting with lights and music, and choosing props. They also design and make costumes and practice with the makeup.

Create a backstage by hanging a backdrop or standing a large cardboard divider behind the stage so the actors can pick up their props and have a place to sit when they are not on stage. Another idea is to use a door for entrances and exits. Instead of opening and closing a curtain, someone can flick the lights in the room on and off to signal that a scene has ended and a new one is about to begin.

The stage manager is responsible for making sure that all the sound and light cues and the scene changes happen at the right time.

The backstage crew is responsible for controlling the lighting board or switches, curtain, and prop table. The backstage crew can also be understudies in case anyone in the cast gets sick.

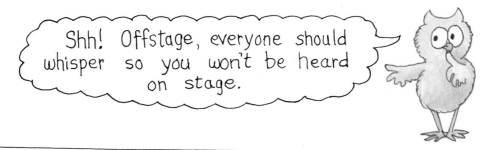

Shh! Offstage, everyone should whisper so you won't be heard on stage.

If you want to change to a new scene, you can also have someone walk across the stage carrying a sign that says where the next scene takes place.

When all the scenery, props, and costumes are ready and the actors know their lines, the cast and crew are ready for the dress rehearsal. This is their chance to act as if an audience is sitting before them, watching.

PUBLICITY

When the sets are created, the technical crew can gather and create signs and flyers to publicize the play. Choose one picture illustrating the theme or plot of your play to go on all the signs. Make the title of the play in large print, and be sure to include the time, date, and place of the performance.

STEP SIX

PERFORM THE PLAY

It's opening night! Assemble the cast early. Then dim the lights and let the curtain go up. Remember, you're there to have fun.

Even with lots of rehearsals, sometimes things go wrong. A prop is missing, a light doesn't go on, or an actor misses a line. Don't panic. Listen for cues. If a mistake is made, the actor should always stay in character. Don't giggle or interact with the audience. Move on!

BREAK A LEG! is the way people wish one another luck in the theater.

A prompter stands off-stage with a script and gives actors help if they forget their lines.

At the end of the play, during the applause, the supporting characters come out first. They stand center stage for a few moments, bow, and then move to the side. Next come the main characters in order of importance. After all the actors are on stage, the director and playwright come forward to also take a bow.

When the play is finished, throw a cast party! Celebrate and talk over the play with your actors and your crew. Make sure everyone who was involved with the play is invited. Congratulations. When the curtain comes down, the actors have gone home, the props are returned to their places, and the theater is empty, step forward. Take a bow. You're now a playwright who has had your work produced.

TAKE A BOW

The theater seats are empty,
The stage is dark and bare.
The audience has gone away,
Applause lingers in the air.

Your play has made a journey
From an idea to the stage.
You did your work, achieved your goal.
You're a playwright come of age.

Through characters, motives, and plotting,
The who, and why, and how.
Step forward as a writer.
As a playwright, take a bow.

Speaking dialogue and using actions
A speech or raised eyebrow.
You made your character come alive,
As an actor, take a bow.

You created a day in the country,
With a backdrop, dress, and plow.
For making sets and costumes,
As a stage hand, take a bow.

Then one last time step forward,
Come on, please do it now.
For setting your goal and achieving it
As a winner, take a bow.

SAMPLE SCRIPTS

The following pages include excerpts of five different types of plays:

 Monologue

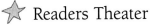 Readers Theater

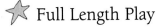 Radio Play

 Full Length Play

Musical Play

Use these as examples to format your own play.

SAMPLE MONOLOGUE

SCIENCE EXPERIMENTS WITH BEN FRANKLIN
by Donna Guthrie

Introduction of Ben Franklin by Teacher

BENJAMIN FRANKLIN

Thank you, thank you, Madam. That was a most gracious introduction.

(To children)

I must admit, I find it peculiar to have a woman teaching school. And there are so many girls in this class. Unusual, very unusual. Not that I mind, of course, but in my time girls weren't permitted to go to school and most teaching was done at home. And a woman schoolmaster would have been most unseemly!

(Laughs)

Your kind schoolmistress invited me here today to instruct you in the natural laws of science and I hope that during this time I might show you some of my inventions.

Inventions, how I love to invent things. By any chance are there any young inventors here today?

(Children answer and have an opportunity to talk about things they have invented.)

As a young lad in Boston, I was always interested in inventions. I think I had a thirst for knowledge that was unusual for a boy my age. I was born on January 17, 1706. The Queen of England firmly ruled the colonies and my father, Josiah Franklin, firmly ruled his house on Milk Street in Boston.

I was one of seventeen children. My mother Abiah was my father's second wife. His first wife died shortly after my father arrived in America. She had seven children.

My father was a soap and candle maker, a good, hard working, honest man who led us all to church three times each Sunday.

My father wished for me to be a minister, but my family was too poor to send me to college. I mastered reading at the early age of five and I could write by seven. My father sent me to school when I was eight. In those days many children never went to school at all. Some went for a year or two and then they started working.

I loved to read but I fear that ciphers, um, mathematics that is, remained a mystery to me. I read all of my father's books. I borrowed books, and whenever I had a bit of money, I spent it on books.

I particularly liked to read books that could teach me something. Do any of you young ladies and gentlemen swim?

(Children answer)

I learned to swim from a book.

I remember the book well. It was called *The Art of Swimming*. It was one of my favorite books.

Well, I don't like to brag, but I could do more than just plain swimming. I could swim backwards, in a circle, underwater, and I could swim with my legs and arms tied together. Never both at once, of course. I would then sink like a stone. It's a law of natural science!

Ah, that was a fine book, *The Art of Swimming*, but sometimes I didn't learn things from any book.

For example, one day I was flying my kite near a swimming pond where we boys used to go. Girls didn't swim of course; it was considered unladylike.

As I said, I was flying a kite and I decided to go for a swim. So I tied my kite to a pole, took off all my clothes, and jumped into the water.

After I swam about for a while, I decided I wanted to fly my kite once again. So I got out of the water and untied my kite and took it into the water with me. Before I knew it, the wind had caught the kite and pulled the kite and me clear across the pond. Oh, how the lads laughed when they saw my new invention.

(Play continues...)

SAMPLE READERS THEATER

SONG OF THE OPEN ROAD
by Jean Ciavonne

CAST:
KATE
BECKY
CRAIG

KATE: Song of the Open Road

BECKY: by Jean Ciavonne

KATE: What time is it, Dad?

BECKY: Are we almost there?

CRAIG: Kate's driving me crazy combing her hair.

KATE: We've been driving forever—let's stop for some chow.

BECKY: I'm sure it's my turn for a window seat now.

CRAIG: I am sooo bored.

KATE: Becky's kicking my feet.

BECKY: What time is it now? I'm hungry. Let's eat.

CRAIG: We've played all the games, and the scenery is dumb.

KATE: Oh, gross—Craig's made snakes with his chewed chewing gum.

(End of play)

SAMPLE RADIO PLAY

ADVENTURES WITH COOL CAT
by Katie Hubbs and Sarah Rogers

MUSIC:	INTRODUCTION
SINGERS:	*(Begin singing)*
COOL CAT:	Hi! I'm Cool Cat. A cat detective.
SINGERS:	*(Still singing)*
COOL CAT:	I have one assistant. His name is Fad Ferret, but everyone calls him Sidekick.

Sound Effects (SFX): KNOCKING ON DOOR

COOL CAT:	Yeah, come in. Hey...sidekick.
SIDEKICK:	Bad news, Cool. Sly and his gang got out again.
SINGERS:	*(Snap fingers once in unison)* Meow!
COOL CAT:	That is bad news. How did they get out this time?
SIDEKICK:	No one knows. The door wasn't open or anything.
COOL CAT:	Sounds like a mystery for Cool Cat.
MUSIC	
COOL CAT:	Come on, Sidekick. Let's get in the car.

SFX:	TRIES TO OPEN CAR DOOR WITHOUT SUCCESS
COOL CAT:	What's the holdup, Sidekick?
SIDEKICK:	The door's locked.
COOL CAT:	Well why didn't you say so? Here's the key.
SFX:	RING OF KEYS THROWN, THEN CAUGHT
SIDEKICK:	Thanks.
SFX:	CAR DOOR IS UNLOCKED
SIDEKICK:	Here you go, Cool Cat.
SFX:	RING OF KEYS THROWN, THEN CAUGHT, TWO CAR DOORS OPEN, THEN CLOSE
SIDEKICK:	So, where are we going, Cool Cat?
COOL CAT:	To the town jail.
SFX:	CAR STARTS, THEN DRIVES AWAY
MUSIC	
SFX:	CAR ARRIVES, THEN SHUTS OFF
COOL CAT:	This is it…
SFX:	TWO CAR DOORS OPEN, THEN CLOSE
COOL CAT:	Come on, Fad Ferret.
SFX:	TWO PAIRS OF FOOTSTEPS ON SIDEWALK

(Play continues…)

SAMPLE FULL LENGTH PLAY

THE PRINCESS AND THE STABLEBOY
by Lauren Johnson

CAST
PRINCESS:	Young and smart
STABLEBOY:	Young and smart
KING:	A kingly type
3 COUNSELORS:	Old and gray
GUARD:	A villain
GENIE:	Wild and wonderful
MONSTER:	Scary (played by the Genie)
MAID	

Setting: The throne room of a beautiful castle. A young princess sits studying a map of the world. She is marking a course with pins and lines. Enters her father, the King, followed by his three counselors. A guard stands at attention nearby.

P: Good morning, father. Good morning, counselors. Come and see where I have decided to go on my trip around the world.

K: *(still not quite awake)* Bring me my breakfast! Bring me my coffee! *(a maid appears with a tray)* Now, what is all this about the world?

3rd C: Your daughter has planned a trip for herself, sire. She wishes to see the world.

K: Stuff! Bother the world! We have everything we need right here in my kingdom. Besides, who knows, there may not even be a world out there. Have you ever seen it? Have I ever seen it? Do you know of anyone who has ever seen it? Certainly not!

P: But father, there must be a world out there or there would not be a map of it here in this book. And all the royal sailing ships, surely they have seen some of the world outside our kingdom.

K: They most certainly have not! They are under strict orders not to sail out of sight of the land. If they did, how would they find their way back? Ships are expensive, my daughter. I can't afford to be building new ones just because some foolish captain wishes to see the world—if there is any to see at all!

P: I know there is a world out there and someday I shall see it. I will take my ship, with the very bravest crew, and sail to all these far-away places—you will see, father! I shall return with the finest stories to tell, and all our people shall come from miles around to listen to me tell my tales!

K: Ho, ho, I have a little dreamer here, don't I? No, my girl, you will not return, because you will not be leaving! You are my only daughter, and soon it will be time for you to take a husband, a young nobleman who will someday take my place. Even I can't live forever!

1st C: But sire, don't you think she is still too young to think of marriage?

K: Bother that! Her mother the Queen, God rest her soul, was about her age when we were married.

2nd C: But times have changed, your highness.

K: Oh, times have changed, have they? We'll see about that! Who's king around here anyway? I am!

3 C's: (a chorus) Of course you are, sire.

K: I am, and I'll say when times have changed and when they haven't. Daughter, a week after your birthday you shall be married! I suggest you put your maps aside and start dreaming instead of your future husband, the prince!

P: But father, I don't want to be married! I want to see the world first! Someday perhaps I shall come home and find a husband; but I don't want to live my whole life in this kingdom!

K: (sputtering) Oh, so, the kingdom where you have been born and raised isn't good enough for you now, is that it? This is what comes of giving a girl everything she could possibly want! She becomes willful and disobedient! I say you shall be married and therefore you shall! Who's king around here, anyway?

3C's: Of course *you* are, sire.

P: But father!

(Play continues...)

MR. VANATOLI AND THE MAGIC PUMPKIN SEEDS
by Donna W. Guthrie and Nancy B. Ekberg

CAST
NARRATOR
MR. VANATOLI
MRS. VANATOLI
PIGS (3 or 4)
MR. K
NEWSMAN
NEWSWOMAN
SINGERS (4 or 5)
SEEDS (4 or 5) with baggy orange cloth bodies
STRANGER
MUSICIAN

Setting: A farmyard at the foot of a great mountain. Mr. and Mrs. Vanatoli's house is in the background. There is a pigsty for the pigs, and a background of growing corn, mountains, and cornstalks tied together. There is an area to the right of the house where the magic seeds are tossed and pumpkins can grow.

Time: Present, early autumn.

Scene One

NARRATOR: (*Enters and stands at far left of stage*) Not far from here, where the skies are always blue and the gentle blowing winds are called Chinooks, there is a great mountain. And at the foot of this mountain there is a beautiful little farm where rows of corn grow straight and tall and noisy pigs eat and eat.

(*Enter pigs, to be followed by Mr. and Mrs. Vanatoli*)

NARRATOR: This little farm is owned by Victor Vanatoli, who is known far and wide as a very practical man.

Practical Man

Recorder alone

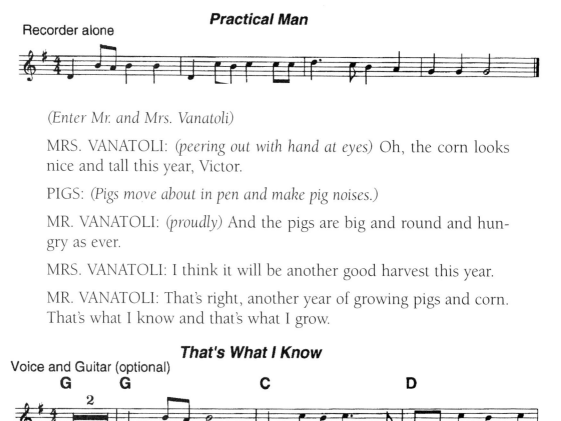

(Enter Mr. and Mrs. Vanatoli)

MRS. VANATOLI: *(peering out with hand at eyes)* Oh, the corn looks nice and tall this year, Victor.

PIGS: *(Pigs move about in pen and make pig noises.)*

MR. VANATOLI: *(proudly)* And the pigs are big and round and hungry as ever.

MRS. VANATOLI: I think it will be another good harvest this year.

MR. VANATOLI: That's right, another year of growing pigs and corn. That's what I know and that's what I grow.

That's What I Know

Voice and Guitar (optional)

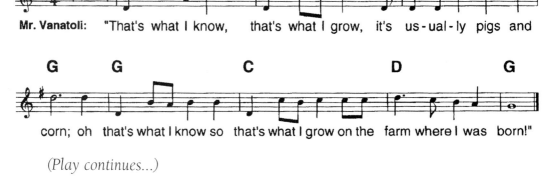

Mr. Vanatoli: "That's what I know, that's what I grow, it's us-ual-ly pigs and

corn; oh that's what I know so that's what I grow on the farm where I was born!"

(Play continues...)

INDEX